STAY

STAY

TANYA OLSON

YESYES BOOKS *Portland*

COVER ART: POLAROID OF HETTIE GARNER PITTARD HART,
© 1976 CHARLES LINWOOD HART
COVER & INTERIOR DESIGN: ALBAN FISCHER

EARLY EDITION AVAILABLE ONLY THROUGH YESYES BOOKS AND THE AUTHOR.
ISBN 978-1-936919-65-9
PRINTED IN THE UNITED STATES OF AMERICA

PUBLISHED BY YESYES BOOKS
1614 NE ALBERTA ST
PORTLAND, OR 97211
YESYESBOOKS.COM

KMA SULLIVAN, PUBLISHER
JOANN BALINGIT, ASSISTANT EDITOR
STEVIE EDWARDS, SENIOR EDITOR, BOOK DEVELOPMENT
ALBAN FISCHER, GRAPHIC DESIGNER
COLE HILDEBRAND, SENIOR EDITOR OF OPERATIONS
JILL KOLONGOWSKI, MANAGING EDITOR
BEYZA OZER, EDITOR, SOCIAL MEDIA
AMBER RAMBHAROSE, EDITOR, ART LIFE & INSTAGRAM
CARLY SCHWEPPE, ASSISTANT EDITOR, *VINYL*
PHILLIP B. WILLIAMS, COEDITOR IN CHIEF, *VINYL*
AMIE ZIMMERMAN, EVENTS COORDINATOR
HARI ZIYAD, ASSISTANT EDITOR, *VINYL*

Dear Emily,–

Are you there, and shall you always stay there, and is it not dear Emily any more,
but Mrs Ford of Connecticut, and must we stay alone, and will you not come back
with the birds and the butterflies, when the days grow long and warm?

—Emily Dickinson, letter to Mrs. Gordon L. Ford
   1853

for Susan

Contents

STAY

Zeno's Boat

On tumorous claws rats boarded the ship
They left their mothers behind That glossy hawk
kept tethered to deck He left his mother behind
Clinging fleas dirt and mites showed resilience
Leaving mothers behind Viruses persevered
in the blood And left their mothers behind

But mothers never forgive departures
A leaving is an arrow to your poor mother's heart
Mothers' hearts hold their young
the way young boys hold birds By a string
kept in hand With a string looped in knot

And children never forget the holding
The strength in mother's grip
comes from fine-tuning bows Underfoot
calloused rats gnaw through a box
as they eat what we carefully stored

From the masts we have spotted the inland pines
But know we will never arrive They are deep
indigenous giants We know we shall

never arrive We pray one day those towers
might fall And know we will never
arrive Miles to yards to feet to inches
Yet we know we can never arrive

Bartholomew the cobbler's son leads the group
through vespers tonight *Though your sins*
be as scarlet I will make them like snow
And ashore wave the long-leaf pines
Behind us bob a string of days
linking *stay* to *go* Below in the hold
rats swim through bilge like they
swam round their own mothers' bellies

Nothing Left To Burn Down Here

One winter there struck
a terrible storm Snow
then ice Snow then ice
Over and over again
Wind blew drifts Cold
froze them hard Layers
that made everything
impossible No getting
out Nothing to get in
The mother explained
the shortage of fuel oil
How they would live
in one room together Hang
blankets in the doorway
To keep in the heat Eat soup
and porridge for meals The girl
thought they should start a fire
Made a list of what they could
Bust up Burn The kitchen table
Dining room chairs A chiffarobe
That word from a library book
How would they return

library books Until a thaw
A break The mother said
no one had to bathe Everyone
still brushed teeth

The fifth day the father
heated blankets and bricks
in the oven Pressed the blankets
to a second floor window
Until it thawed enough to open
Duct-taped 2 of the bricks to his belly
Zipped coveralls over it all Slid
out the window Down
the drift Dug out the side door
Turned around Tunneled into the snow
Made a room Deep enough
to crawl into Tall enough to sit
For you girls To play in Fresh air
It was better that way Inside
but out Gave them
a lantern to see by
Nothing you could burn down here
The walls grew shiny as they
Melted and froze Melted
And froze again

The girls read books Played TV Show
Charlie's Angels The one where Kelly
gets shot in the head by the sweet simple boy

Who does not understand what a gun is
Can do How beautiful she looks
in the hospital bed The part
where she wakes up Forgives him
Little House on the Prairie
The one where they tie Pa
to the fence Afraid a raccoon
may have given him rabies
How they do not want
to do it How Pa says It is
what they must do Before sleep
that night the sister asked
Do you think that we could do it
Zipped into sleeping bags
Buried under blankets
Ovened bricks against
their feet Tops of their heads
just touching together
Do you really think we could

Before the roads would open again
Before the fuel oil would make it through
Before the father would leave
and return Leave and return again
They slept in their day clothes
Ate off their laps Washed
only hands Talked only
to each other Breathed in
the other's breath

a million times Then a million
times again Swore they would always
live together Just like this In this house
When they were Old Older
Until the day they died
The girls would live
much longer than they imagined
But never again like that
Tunneled in a den
Matted Feral Warm

Did you think that we
could do it I did not
think we could

When Uncle Bruce

When Uncle Bruce was drinking
We fired off the shotgun
at midnight *Aim it high baby girl*
Right there The moon How he
picked you up when it knocked you down
How then it was a new year

When Uncle Bruce was working
It was mostly down the mine
Dark in Dark out Dark all day inside
Roofer when the mine shut down Idled
Can see to can't And I get this handsome tan

When Uncle Bruce was sober
He took you for a drive Just
the two of you Just for fun
Into town In the truck Lucky Strikes
rolled at his bicep Spit cup Balanced
on the transmission in between
Hole rusted in the floorboard

where the cup tipped over again and again
Free air conditioning baby girl
And my socks get clean when it rains

When Uncle Bruce was tired
He sent all the kids to town
The oldest got to drive The youngest
held the money Everyone else
Piled in the back *Count heads*
when you get there Again
before you leave Keep her between
the ditches Keep her out of the fields

When Uncle Bruce was flush
It was pizza night at Angelo's
Quarters to play the jukebox
Each of you gets to choose one
And remember everybody here
has to listen to that song
When *Desperado* came on
Uncle Bruce from across the bar
Who the hell played this

When Uncle Bruce was drinking
He kept a bottle halfway between
home and the mine Tucked behind
a telephone pole Tossed in the field
when it was done Until one day
A finished bottle sat waiting for him

Two notes rolled in its neck
Get yourself some help
and *Keep your goddamn empties*
out of my field

if ghosts

ghosts unable
to cross water ghosts
unable to climb stairs
gravity a stooped ghost
who ferries us home

radar ghosts radio ghosts
sunlight ghostlight
moonlight ghostlight's ghost

pepper's burn ghost
cat's stare ghost
your dead brother
calls your name ghost
in the plane
you're a ghost
trailing behind you
the ghost of a ghost

imagine their number
no wonder we hear them

they feed on our faces
until we become them

a ghost reads this poem
to the ghosts of the poem
a mother ghost
a father ghost
hear the leaves rustle
that's a ghost's shuffle

o camerado close!
o you and me at last

dear Mr President

my first plan was Swim to Cuba
since they are the enemy closest at hand
imagine that journey 103 miles
61 hours stingrays jellyfish sharks
the only way anyone ever made it
is locked inside a cage but I
was determined to go armed only
with the heat banked inside
my fiery fiery bones

          the day we got
your letter Mr President I nodded along
with its sympathy until I read
No act of violence
no matter how heinous
can halt the spread of freedom
did you forget how he died
charred abroad returned as a stick

stacked in a hold and handed to a family
who chose to grind him down
and grind him down until all
that was left was a handful of dust
the person who wished most
to hold him whole
just one more time again
had to cast across the water
into a suddenly meaningful breeze

                                    which

leaves me to wonder Mr President what
would have happened if I had said
Don't Go surely a boy can hear
his sister's *Don't Go* through
the rah rah all around surely
he listens for a *Don't Go* inside
each *Thank You For Your Service*
behind an *Active Duty Boarding First*
but I never said it *Please Don't Go* I guess
no one else did either

                        my next plan Mr President
began with the *Leaves of Grass*
somebody left on the bus did you know
Walt himself came to Washington
after reading in the paper his brother
had been shot at Fredericksburg he stared
into wounded face after wounded face

until George was finally the one looking back
when George got better and returned to war
Walt stayed to help other hurt boys
sat with them sang to them
wrote their letters home in one
he called grass *the beautiful uncut*
hair of graves can you imagine
writing such a thing Mr President
can you imagine being the mother
to read it Walt stayed and wrote
and stayed and wrote until he himself
had a terrible stroke and this time
it was George who came to fetch Walt
and tenderly bear him home

                                      writing is all
Walt had to get him through the war
and writing is how he realized
every last molecule of every dead being
still lives in existence somewhere
that every face he ever saw
he would see in some other face again
at first I kept all his letters in a box
tied it shut swore I would never read them
until he came home safe turns out
he signed each one *Now You Stay Sweet*
made sure to leave out the ugly

                                    I glimpse him
some mornings in the woods out back
he's dimming drifting further away I wrote
him down Mr President so you
carry him now say his name hold him close
feel his weight give him space a wasp
upon your tongue

ever you desire

fly to me ride to me
home from the island

how simple how soon
will your dearness

be home what comes
to the island must leave

the island what leaves the island
drifts back ashore coming

and going the island serves music
all the pretty boys play

all the pretty songs the birds
offer *jug jug* the boys offer

jug jug Me say war jug jug
Everywhere war so simple

so soon throats open together
a hunger a cackling fly away

home which is to say the birds
are flocking outside our window

which is to say swooning
at the pane the cat sings *jug jug*

Gladys Seated Next To Me At The Bar

Turns Nods Says *Can't remember*
if you lost yours yet Salutes the air
with her bottle *but my own dad*
passed this morning Lowers
the bottle Pulls at the neck *Lay there*
for weeks Never moved Nothing
to say Until today Opened his eyes
Dark side of dark Spoke as clear
as day 'There's the big ship
come for me Guess it's time
to go' Raises the bottle
to order again *And that*
as they say was that

I close the sports section Offer
condolences My own story A morning
I was maybe 12 How my mother
entered the room Woke me Edge
of the bed Hand through
my hair Then in my hand
Its tender tightening A gentle squeeze
Then her story Of the UFO How it

came in the night 3 sharp knocks
On the roof In the air
A feeling she called
Strangely Compelled
To go outside Stand in the yard
Look up A V-shape of green lights
below a white one so bright
she first thought it the moon Swore
I couldn't leave you I never would
Though of course In the end She did
Asked if I Heard Anything Saw
Anything Anything Odd at all
Not to be frightened Just to tell her
Promised her I hadn't
Though of course I had

Gladys nods Thumbs the quarters
in front of her *Wheel in a wheel*
in a wheel in a wheel Just like
in the Bible Says *Twice I saw*
my daddy cry Both times
it was here First When Earnhardt
hit the wall Then when Junior won
Same race Same track
3 years to the day
Only sport he ever cared about
Go fast Turn left
Fathers chasing sons

Pulled the quarters into a stack
in front of her *Go play*
us some jukebox Dolly
First with Porter Then alone
Tuesday's Gone Blaze of Glory
Something Bocephus Something
by his daddy That new one
where the mouthy girl sings
'I said I wouldn't do it
But I did it again'

54 Prince

There exist 54 Goldilocks planets
54 planets not too hot
54 planets not too cold
54 planets where the living
is juuuuuust right
in that particular planetary zone

So 54 planets like Earth
But not Earth Similar
Not the same 54 planets close
but different Different
except for Prince

I Would Die For You Prince
Purple Rain Prince
Paisley Park Prince
Ejaculating Guitar Prince
High-Heel Boots Prince
Assless Pants Prince
Knows He's In The Truth Prince
Won't Salute The Flag Prince
Doesn't Believe In Time Prince

Wrote *Slave* Upon His Face Prince
Took An Unpronounceable Symbol For His Name Prince
Chka Chka Chka Ahh Prince

54 planets Each with a Prince
And every Prince exactly the same
as the one we know here on Earth
54 lace 54 canes
54 planets 54 Prince

These 54 Prince eat
54 of our worries The 54 worries
become 54 songs 54 songs
made of 54 bars 54 bars
using 54 chords 54 downbeats
where the Prince pick up
the worries 54 off-beats
to lay the worries down again
54 worriful skank-beat Prince
birth 54 worrisome funk-drenched songs

Birthed of these songs
the Prince gather round Lake Minnetonka
When the cherry moon smiles
they thrust under their heads
Into the waters they sick up
our old worries Freed of our worries
the Prince grow ready again

It takes a worried man the Prince say
to sing a worried song
While under the waters of Lake Minnetonka
the bass in their holes
and the gobies in the shoals
Swarm around our used worries
Nibble at our old worries
My stepsister wants the shoe
to fit her worries I swapped the cow
for a handful of beans worries Grandma
oh Grandma what big teeth you have worries
I been left in the forest by my bad parents
worries Skimmed from the top
worries Scraped from the bottom
worries Spooned from the middle
just good enough worries
There's worries now the fish sing
but there won't be worries long

Sometimes Birds Spontaneously

Heal their wings
Handle it themselves
The Chinese New Year
Another hop around the sun
Left wing held out Away
Until it heals Feels better
Fold it in Take flight

Accuse another bird
Of witchcraft Sorcery
That bird implicating
another I Saw You
On the back of that fox
In the clearing The one
where the circus appears
Confession recanted
Red Fire Monkey Year done

Stay when they ought
to go Winter over
Stall the departure Neglect
to molt Practice a song

Practice again Then
In the end Sing it not

Leave together All
at once On healed
wings With a lightening
sun In the air
Their song Sung
in the harmony of birds *It'll be*
no more the water
Gonna be the fire
next time

First American

When I am the first
of the Female American Suicide Bomber team
to go I will request the trigger
that detonates upon release
Not the one you have to press down
I am good at this My job
I see it happen before it does
These the images that carry me
to sleep Where a redbird flutters
Perched atop my heart The song
he sings for me A song I hum
just to him Making me believe
if I can get within 20 feet I can surely
get within 10 And if I
can get within 10 feet
Nothing will stop me from 5
And 5 feet means I can touch him
Cup his fleshy chin Drag
a path down his caked face
Better that way So his sorrows
might leave him Or perhaps
I will wait until he sleeps Click

the TV off Lift the sheet Crawl in
behind Tuck his buttocks in my lap Top
my arm across his girth Pull him to me
until our hearts are aligned Cup his breast
Thumb the nipple Sing *This
is what it's been like What every day
has been like* Then Release
How we vaporize Almost
together Deadman's switch
they call it Giving in Letting go
What every day has been like

Things Like Words
Words Like Things

Emily Dickinson to Joseph Cornell

May 3rd, 1886

I'm so accustomed to my Fate
You and I asleep Like Trailing Arbutus
Our hidden nest Cheek to Dirt
A Plant returns Its Letter from Spring
And these Boxes Yours to me

I am not used to Hope
Come for dinner Veal Shanks
in Marrow Brioche ordered
the day before And Apricots
Though as Father notes
Like penitent Girls
There soon will be no more

Sheep Boy of Templeogue

Mammy said was the sidhe
Took Baby Frances
Left Simple Francie behind
Took Lovely Daddy
Put Quiet Da in his boots

I used to tell how
the sidhe carrying me
Got caught out by dawn
Had no choice but to lay me down
Beneath the hawthorne tree
For the Guards to find at full light
Beautiful she was Tall and graceful
With pointy ears Gentle
when she left me Weeping
when she walked away

Better I remember the judge
You are to mind the Brothers now
Don't they know best
for a boy like you
Was the Brothers warned us

No lamb is ever spared
the unblinking eye of God

A likely story Children
that is today Girls giggling
Pinching their nose
Boys swearing Daring each other
A hundred quid if you walk home
the Sheep Shaggers way You know
he kills any who spy him at a sheep
The lip of the bold ones now
And no one notices a thing

Not as it was then The day Mossie
and me went on the hop
to the fair Skint But your man
out front eyed us whispering
Artane boys do get in free A hand
on the neck A shove in the tent
Get a good eyeful Specky
You'll think twice
before leaving those walls again

But it was nothing
Just a Sheep Boy inside
A boy been raised by sheep
Left maybe or wandered away
Taken in by sheep what fed him
Milk with the lambs I suppose

Knees calloused white
from crawling Wrists splayed
Thicker than thighs
Long matty fur all over his back
A pull at his ear for a wet horn bleat
Uncanny and forlorn

There are devils to roam
this quare round world and they
sing you their songs for free
But that was just a boy
with the face of a boy
Like Francie or Mossie or me

A Ship What Set To Sea

Imagine a boat leaves shore Its home Where it was made Born First time asea Maiden
voyage Made to be sent to war Before it's even beyond sight of land her first board breaks
Broken by Able-Seaman Johnson Tried to stomp a rat Missed And the board snapped
in two Johnson a well-fed country boy Never truly clear on what he had signed
up to do Spent his days Seasick Homesick Until the skirmish where he took one to the
vitals The doctor called it *a through and through* So the carpenter sends his nimble
apprentice deep into the hold Oversees the boy Choosing a board Sizing it right Planing
it smooth Monitors as he hammers it in place Nods his head Approves And every day
means some other need Some other nail Some other board The sail finally too torn to be
mended made bandages be the doctor's son *Assistant* his father calls him His mother calls
him stolen No bandage wasted on Johnson No recovery from a through and
through None for the carpenter's apprentice Hung off the side for repairs Dashed
by one rogue wave *Man overboard* cried the carpenter But the ship She never slowed
The apprentice taken by the sea And the carpenter's good hammer too When a city
breaks one layer gets poured atop another over and over again But a ship needing repair
must create each layer anew From its stores at first of course But then Improvisation
Some sense of how to Make do Nails shaped into bullets A hat forced to do for a shoe
So who could argue the ship that left port is the same one still now at sea Surely not the
doctor's wife She bore herself a brand new son This one with skyblue eyes Certainly not
the carpenter Who right now himself is replacing yet another board with his supposedly
second-best hammer

txt me im board

I monitor my nephew's Instagram
Call it *Being responsible* Say *His*
own best interests Never *Stalking*
Not *Invasion* Not *Spying* Not really
Nearly every picture a selfie
Him 12 Slumped Staring
Rilly board txt me And he
looks bored too That teenage look
Set mouth Hard eyes
Fending off Girding for battle
It breaks my heart
Him practicing this
His trying it on

Today I watch
from 30,000 feet thanks to
Gogo Inflight Internet and Allstate Insurance
30 minutes free in exchange
for my email and phone number
That's not really me I think
and hit Agree Nick
he likes to go by now But I

still call him Nicholas He is
board just chillin in the basement
What sometimes he calls
his *Man Cave* And I could
contact him from here The Sky
But he doesn't mean me He wants
his friends *My bros My boys*
And soon enough probably
Girls One already leaves
ur a babe so hot Others
Heart it for Like So now
they are practicing that too
And you can see the need
to monitor words not meant
for me He wants to talk
to ones who are bored
And me I am not bored I am
flying A window seat Country
unrolling slow below

                  I am flying
east From San Francisco
Where I spent the week reading
with the same three poets every night
Every night we read together
Every night we said our words
It moved me Our time together
What they dared to say
and because of them I grew less afraid

Let me call them by their names
Roger Reeves Matt Hart Phillip B Williams
What a sausage-fest I thought at first
But seven nights I heard
their words From that
I came to love them

The man
in the middle seat though is frightened
He is rocking Sweating *A stranger*
I left A stranger I return he prays
Hands cupped before his eyes
The flight attendant gives him water
Just think of the air as an ocean
And the turbulence that's just waves
But it doesn't help He is
rocking still Sweating still
Is praying Is nervous Not me
I am flying And when flying
I pull on my *I'm not angry*
I'm not brown face as soon
as I enter the airport Pull on my
Trust me I'm really a woman face
Wear it the flying day through
My wrists might get swiped
Upper arms patted But not
All of me Not pulled aside
Not stripped Hair never
fingered I may be a girl

who looks like a boy
But bathrooms in the air
aren't sexed yet Up here
I don't count as Dangerous

                Since

Nicholas was young he has always
loved games Monopoly Uno Little kid
versions But even more so Talking Games
I Spy What Begins With
I'm Going On A Picnic
His favorite for a while
we invented one day
Bored Raining Took turns asking
What Would You Save
From This Burning Room
His first answers always toys
Thomas SpongeBob My cat
Murphy the first living thing
he ever named 5 maybe
And I thought One day
he will become some sort of man
What do you think Murphy would save
I asked Gravely he nodded
Murphy would save me

                I turn

to the window Pop in earbuds
Those little marshmallows In them

a woman sings along with
a racking shotgun Below me
Everything has gone Ice and Hard
Rock and Hard Colorado maybe
Maybe Nevada Something licked
a mountain up here Someone
had to be the first to cross it Someone
the first to see it from above Now
in that mountain Young men and women
sit locked inside Staring at screens
Where they must see what I see now
Road and Stone Scrub and Stone
Every thing a thing People
just assumed And the young
Men and Women (Soldiers I guess)
toggle sticks and switches
Trying to kill people Who aren't
at that same moment
Actively trying to kill them
War now War then War here
a war there *War* hippies
in San Francisco used to say
is not healthy for children
and other living things

                    Nicholas
used to tell me *I think I'll serve*
my country by being helpful
Pick up litter maybe Maybe

pet shelter dogs But now he posts logos
Army Strong The Few The Proud
to his Instagram His Social Studies
teacher told the class *My first time*
you would hear the bombs
before you saw them (And here
Nicholas traces an arc through the air
while he whistles a dying whistle)
But the next time through
it was all IEDs His Social Studies teacher
told the class *They ought to let me*
first on the plane because
I teach you monkeys Not
because I got sent to war
In my earbuds the woman sings
along to an AK sound Makes melody
from its *blat blat blat*

                  Our last evening
together Matt Hart announced *So far*
I've cried three times today Once
at the ocean Once during the reading
Just now standing at the bar
Down below Mountains have stopped
The Earth has gone flat
Giant circles Patchwork farmland
Food in America Visible from above
Allergies I explain to the man in the middle
as I decline the offered peanuts He shrugs

If God has written 'You will die in a desert'
It is in the desert you will die
He keeps his eyes out the window
Seems to be feeling better Everyone
is sleeping reading snacking watching football
What can't you do from the sky these days
It is quiet in here Surely outside
we must be loud Clouds look
full fluffy bitable Surely
they are not

Before I left
I told Nicholas about Murphy
How she went out late one night
and never came back home
No sign of a scuffle I never
heard a sound He sighed heavy
I been knowing that cat
my whole life Texted later
Gonna fine that kayot
Cut opin his stomik
Give Murphy back 2u
He can't spell Dear God
None of them can spell anymore
What do they do all those
hours in school Beneath the plane
Clouds make a floor Around the plane
Clouds build their house

Under us
somewhere The Mississippi A mile wide
they say Where Something once
licked the land in two Someone once
was the first to cross it Someone first
eyed it from above Coffee soda snacks
roll through Clouds pull in Closer still
Form buffalo circles Bulls to the outside
Calves and sows tucked away inside
A form they use to fend off wolves How do
soldiers know when to Pull the trigger
Toggle the switch Push the button
(I have no idea how we fire
what we use as guns anymore)
How does anything look dangerous
from here How does everything
not Each night Roger Reeves read
Even the lions have left
for the mountains Each night he read
Most young kings come home
without their heads Our president
keeps a list of people he thinks
should be killed Nicholas's whole life
has been during war People on the list
are Scratched off Erased Nicholas
only sees dead bodies on his screen
where a death grants him another life
The president's list never grows
any shorter Outside the plane

Clouds even closer Beyond
the plane Clouds darker still

                              The man
on the aisle turns on his light Neither
the man in the middle nor I like this
Makes it impossible to see out the window
A voice breaks in Around us Above us
We're going to put a hold
on service right now I'll ask
everyone to please return
to their seats Buckle in
We show turbulence ahead
And it looks like it will be
with us the whole way home
The man in the middle grows paler
again I wonder if now is the time
to bring this poem to a stop Write
Nicholas a note instead *You*
are my most favorite person ever
You carried me from all my burning rooms
But it is impossible to write
as the plane Drops then Rises
Lowers one side Lowers the other
This is not the ocean
says the man in the middle
Air is not the ocean at all
We touch shoulders over
and over as we rock side

to side I push myself back
into the seat Close my eyes

Phillip

usually came last to breakfast Scuffled
in slippers Fuzzled by sleep A dancer
first Of course then Royal Of course
looking Regal Cloaked in a bathrobe
he carried across the country
just for moments like this A wise
Prince rehearses the weight
of wearing King We drop more
Faster this time Everyone *Woahs* together
Except for the man in the middle
Who is smiling Who pats my hand
Have no fear my friend Wisest uncle
Pats twice again *God takes no poet
until his best poem is written
You my friend will save us all*
And truly he believes this
For he never stops smiling Not
as the turbulence worsens
Not when it grows worse again
Not when everyone folds
themselves in two Not as
all of us drop head to knees
Not when lightning strikes us
Not as I taste us burn

We land of course Planes always do
Every chicken returns to her roost
Still everyone claps at touch down
The man in the middle palms
the top of my head *You did it*
my friend Brought us all back home
We sit blinking at each other
in a red light swirl Our plane
alone Away from the airport
And I no longer see them
But I can hear them still
Engines screaming Thrusts reversing
The screeching kiss when
the tires hold A song that promises
Yet another Someone
is given Yet another Chance
To make their very own
God Marked Best Poem

Meep Meep

Wile E seen what he see
Throaty coyote Yellow juice eyes
Seen the man eyeball him
Eyeballs on Eyeballs off
Coyote know when
disrespect enough
Coyote predator All the rest
prey Pity man run Man run
Coyote chase Coyote chase
Coyote catch Coyote love
the tackle Coyote love a struggle
Coyote love knee to the back
Elbow in kidney Love forearm
on head Coyote love living
up top Coyote love prey
beneath him

Every man got it Animal inside
Coyote Tiger Whale Bear Most time
it lay sleeping Curled up Dreaming
But animals sleep light Wile E
rest One eye cracked Ready

44

Twitchy coyote Juice yellow eyes
Weight on what he holding Muzzle
to cheek Hot breath in the ear
Say it again motherfucker
Say meep meep again

Someday I'll Love Ocean Vuong

We sit drenched The rotten mouth
of spring That stench of its too full

flowers To live Learn to breathe
with your mouth full of Dead

Bulge out your cheeks Strain out
their bones Remember the teeth

They are our most apparent
skeleton The first time I drank

Kombucha I did not think
I should swallow this Feckless

hippies Their piss vinegar The way
they pass around their pussy mothers

Finally Tongue out the organs Cast
these to the page Link them They make

a Poem Ocean told me what I call Chocolate
is nothing but rotted cacao Liquified

Fermented Set to solid again Yikes Bite
out his rooted tongue Chocolate Coffee

The end of my vices Someday
they will cost me But Somewhere

you have to draw a line Someday
I might drink again They say

You have to say that But I Won't
Couldn't How much more now

I feel My first thought on drinking
Kombucha was *This is some seriously*

rancid White People Shit Instead of *pussy*
you're meant to write *purulent* For instance

Pus suppurates from her purulent sores
Punctuation the way we show what's gone

What's missing In my ears a family
harmonizes *Hang me Oh Hang me*

I'll be dead and gone Out of me Poems
eke upwards In me Poems pool on the tongue

Ocean said *Stuff the tiny fish head down*
in a sack Hang them in the sun Gather

their drippings Voila Fish Sauce To love
sit down to a plate full of dead Lower

your mouth Shovel them in Slurp
them like noodles Aerate Swallow

Scrape the leftbehind film
from your tongue That aftertaste

is Love My nephew is the end
of our Olsons The North Star

to which we've always
been running All childhood

I feared he would drown The end
now looks more like a flame Why

would I ask to be put in a Box
Liquify Emulsify Seep through

the cracks Instead Slip me
in the sea SkyBurial BodyFarm

Excarnation whatever way we best
know how Left no other choice

Burn these Sugar Bones When I go
Let it be gagging on a mouthful

of everyone I love The acid of them
Their tongueless moans Cast these

to the page My final poem Ocean says
Push your poem to a point of failure

Now Push it a little more The family
in my ears agrees *You know it's not*

so much the hanging It's the laying
in the grave so long I inherit

the inadequacies of a father Someday
I'll learn Not to nourish them Not to plant

them deep Buried in six foot rows
Someday I won't water them daily

Leave their angry fruit Adangle Alone
In the end I'll miss the bitter

of chocolate The bite of its bean Dark
Coffee Cream One day you grow

Sick and Tired of being Sick and Tired
A Saying for Brains too liquid

to think Drinking is just Drowning
While you're still standing up If I live

another life Let me live it in a body Sink me
in the ocean Cast me on the air There will

probably be no one to do this for me
But Nicholas That's what it means

to go extinct *I had an aunt* he'll say
She loved me so much she and name

something I likely never did
Keep this poem from him Float it out

to sea Bury it in a book Ocean told me
I'm definitely going to use that fish sauce

story in a poem Stolen With his *Yikes*
Taken for my own Pile my leftovers

Higher Wider than I stand now Bones Teeth
Poems Soak them in liquor Set them aflame

All my failures I grew to know Punctuation
a way I try to claim what I own

My fermenting teeth My wet dry love
Our moment of too full flowers

Echoes Require A Space Between

from here it sounds romantic
muffled thuds like quilted bombs
but you insist *Can you hear that*
It's almost 11 I could be sleeping
and hold the phone up to the window
where through the speaker now I hear
echoing cracks and sharper explosions
a shave of a second before they arrive
at my own home edges dulled by the
not quite a mile they traverse
only sound travels faster than sound
and we discuss how ballparks
often end up on the poorer side
of town departing friends
finishing books writer's block
I confess when a poem is done
I sometimes think *That may be the end*
of that but never really panic for there
is no echo from the well when I say it
unlike when we say goodnight and the
summer sky swallows the satellite
so you tell it to me twice slightly altered

deftly paused a little fading *Goodbye*
Goodnight the echo eaten by everything
that comes between us leaving only
revealing remnants of *night* and *bye*

Other People Call It America

The Reverend CL Franklin
rode that Great Migration
right out of Sunflower County
Car then bus Bus then train
Memphis Buffalo Detroit
Told the word as God revealed it
A fiery word of God The building
word of God Let God's word build
Until it broke Washover
the heads of his little ones
Carl Erma Carolyn Aretha
A wave that left them washed
in the word That wave
left those children anointed

That same migration
left the Townsends behind
Rose up plenty But the
Townsend family stayed
All 20 children stayed
Stayed to Sunflower County
Stayed to sharecropping

Stuck on Marlow land
Strong family Mighty children
Each one pick a couple hundred
pounds a day Every day But Sunday
Sunday Go To Meeting Day
Sunday for Wearing the Crown
Sunday All about the Glory
Meeting the place Fannie Lou met Pap

Aretha wanted to cross over
But not really leave Go
But take the gospel with her
Took a lot with her from the gospel
What a hat and fur
say about a woman
Why it's smart to get
the cash up front
Stash the cash in your purse
Prop the purse up top the piano
Where the purse can always be seen
Wear a fur to show
You conquered this world
Drop the fur to show
You can leave this world behind

Ms Hamer wish to speak true
Make the world say
what it said Give up
what it done Took her purse

with her to testify For what
was in it For what it said
about her Said *My name*
is Mrs Fannie Lou Hamer
Said *I live at 626*
East Lafayette Street
Ruleville Mississippi
Said *I question America*
Said *16 bullets was fired*
into the home for me
Said *Our lives be threatened daily*
Purse say *Sunflower County*
Ms Hamer said *Is this America*

Ms Hamer spoke this
to America There was only
3 channels back then So everybody
heard it Only 3 channels then
So everybody watch the same thing
Everybody watch it mean Everybody
talk about it Ms Hamer put her purse
up top the table Sat herself behind it
Said these things to America
Everybody Even the president
heard her Ms Hamer and her purse
scare the president so bad
He took her right off the TV

Ms Franklin sang
the first black president
into the White House
Wore her coat Wore her hat
Sang him right in the front door
Hat like a big tied bow
People lined up all down
the Mall Set her purse
on the chair *Watch that*
for me Stood up to sing
Hand on her heart
Land where my father died she sang
Let freedom ring she sang
Let it ring she sang *Let it ring*
My Country 'Tis of Thee
this song is called Other people
call it *America*

That's progress right
Something like it
Ever North Ever North
R-E-S- Detroit
all gutted buildings
R-E-S- Flint awash
in leaded children
Detroit One building aflame
catch up the next
Flint A city left dry at its bones

Ms Hamer buried
in Ruleville now Easy walk
Gravesite to home
Made her house a daycare
I'm sick and tired
the headstone say
of being sick and tired
Ms Franklin sang the other day
at the Kennedy Center
Wore her fur out on to the stage
Put her purse on top the piano
Sat herself down to play
Background singers say *Ah-oop*
President set to crying
Background singers *Ah-oop* again
Honored White Lady
proceed to lose her mind
Ms Franklin stand herself up
Ms Franklin walk away
from that piano Man
come out behind her
Mr Man going to finish
playing this song
You make me feel she sang
And drop her fur to the floor
You make me feel she sang
With her arm rose up in the air
You make me feel she sang
You make me feel

Never Never Pants

The children across the street from me
seldom wear pants Mostly not
Mostly never Some do
Some times Girl pants Boy pants
On girls and boys Sometimes correspondingly
Sometimes not Mostly though
Not pants And one of the passel Never
Hot no pants Cold no pants
Rain no pants Sun no pants
At Halloween they are Pilgrims
He is the Pilgrim without pants
Underwear sure And now
they have a dog But never
never pants

No Pants is also the waver
of the bunch All of them outside
The whole gang together
When I leave he breaks away
Toddles to the fence
Squats a firmer stance
Arms extended Elbows locked

Hands in sync Back and forth
Wipers in a flash spring flood
And I wave too Back at him
Most times Not just some
Such passion Such enthusiasm
The fire inside him for waving
Pants are not the thing that make us

Not that you would know it
by me My pride in growing
split-legged Pride in dropping
the tail Finned myself up
from the ocean Scraped
the scales off my thighs
I only go back now to visit
Of course I wear my pants
Work pants Travel pants
Fat pants Dancing pants
How brattish How juvenile
My dripping pride in pants

Outta Sight

Earth spin slower come summer
Do it again Fridge One more time
Fridge From the top Fridge
Hell son You big enough
Hit the 3 hole and stay there
Stay how man make a dog
forget Forget how close
he live to wolf Close enough
any dog eat any man Stay
train the dog to forget

More time More gravity
come summer Wolf curl
himself round your neck
Muzzle in your ear
Lean in Whisper *die*
Hot breath Off and on
Fur creeping down your throat
Lungs clap Front on back
Heart keep waving
One tired swimmer

Wolf been big

since I was little

After practice though
I go slim Hang old wolf
behind the door Ain't a game
Can't nobody find us Don't
nobody know was me
Untipped the cow
Rehung the peach
Debroke the eggs
Slip the yolk back in its sac
Stroke the shell closed again
Tuck it all up back inside that chicken
Out of sight Out of mind
Wolf round the door once more

Son of a Son of a Son

We are riding the train
We are bobbing our heads
To the chewing gum stuck in our ears
With the marshmallows over our ears
And when we pass the spot
Some of the people point and say
That's where it used to be
My father brother uncle took me there
My grandmother mother teacher took me there
That's when we lived in little houses
And museums were in little houses
mixed in amongst the people
Science I think it was
Science then meant 'animals' and 'weather'
Crazy we ever lived like that
But that was all we knew
Back then everyone had a Kickstarter
Back then Something to do with cigarettes
Something because of tobacco

Later that evening my wife and I say
I go there sometimes

And it's like it was then
It's not exactly like a dream
And my wife and I say *I can see it still*
As if it was there
It's not exactly like a dream

The information in our ears
directs us to look to the other side
Dinosaurs lived there one time
Big ones and little together
Sometimes one kind ate another
Then the earth swallowed all the things
and turned them into oil
Our ears say
That's just how Science was back then
And our youngest says It's no fun
Being held and squeezed like that

And then the ride is over
And I put a hand at the back of my wife
And I put a hand on the head of my biggest
And I say *OK Now* and we pull
The chewing gum out of our ears
Take the marshmallows off of our ears
And we chew and chew and chew
And on the count of three
Swallow all of it down
But Science says you can't swallow
and keep your eyes open

So I only pretend to swallow my own
Eyes open Adam's apple Up then Down
Just like my father used to do
Just like his father before him

In A World Only A Little Different

In a world only a little different
both my parents are still living
She died She died and the bruise
lifted from her and slid inside me
She died and there was nowhere
to talk to her but inside my head
He died He died and instantly
I was gone Tracking chip
pulled Location services disabled
I cannot find where they live now
In the world I mostly live in
I wander Bruised Unseen

What I wish for What I wish for most
is one more day I wish for a world
where I could pay a year of my life
and get one more day with them
My father would go to work *I haven't
come all this way to sit around the house
all day* (and today let's keep him happy)
and my mother and I would have coffee
and talk and go to lunch and talk

and share our food and talk
and I would tell her about
my life now How I write now
How I love now Outside myself now
And these would be words
And they would be
In the world Not in my head
And some of the words
would make questions Questions
about her About her life About
how she felt During this During that
She would speak And I would listen
And I would hear her real voice
Speaking aloud Not in my head
And my father My father would come home
and we would have dinner *At the table*
I have not come this far to eat
in front of a TV And I would set it
(the table) and my father would be
in his recliner while my mother
would cook Meatloaf maybe Maybe
fried chicken A pitcher of tea
Wilted cabbage Cucumbers
and onions (It may as well
be summer The garden may as well
be full) And we will eat together
and talk of our day And there will be
more talking More words Slowly
a tick-tock will grow louder By the end

we will be shouting She and I
will try to squeeze in a last few words
We will be shouting to hear
our last words over the louder and louder
tick-tock And then they will
be gone My parents will be gone
And once again there will be
no words

Allow us this One more day
As we were As we truly were
Short Flawed Doing the best
we could When they are gone
I hold only their absence
Absent I hold only her bruise
And with a year subtracted from me
I would offer up another
And this world would be only
a little different

Bobby Bare

My mother seldom drank
but there may have been
drink taken the night
she accosted Bobby Bare
in the bar of The Derby
the place in town you went
if you didn't want pizza
A night out No kids
And there was Bobby Bare
Now Bobby Bare America
is one of your finest song interpreters
Things Change How I Got To Memphis
500 Miles Streets of Baltimore
Though probably he got richest
from *Drop Kick Me Jesus*
Through The Goalposts Of Life
A song not as funny as you think
it might be A song Bare sang
Straight Respectful Bare Senior
I might note As Bobby Bare Junior
also makes his living as a musician
Though Junior himself admits

My dad is three times
the singer I am So you can imagine
my mother's surprise at running into
a Great American Artist in the bar
of The Derby A place mostly known
as the Home of the Horseshoe
an open-faced sandwich consisting
of meat french fries and hot liquid cheese
Hamburger usually But sometimes
Ham or Pork Tenderloin
Everyone makes it their own way
Everyone thinks theirs is the best
The secret isn't in the meat though
The secret is the Richness of the cheese sauce
the Crispiness of the fries Maybe Bare
ate one If he didn't he should have
Though cheese has been known
to clog a singer's throat Anyway
There she is My mother
Out to dinner When going
out to dinner really meant something
I mean you might grab a hot dog
from the snack bar during Monday Night League
or pizza from Angelo's to mark a child's birthday
But going out out didn't happen often
Which might explain the drink taken
by my seldom-drinking mother Night out
No kids Husband Friends And now this
Right in front of you A man you likely heard

on the radio driving in to town A man
you might have seen on *Hee Haw* Standing
right in front of you *Bobby Bare* she yelled
What are you doing in Taylorville Illinois
Later she found out he was playing
two nights at the Christian County Fair
Saturday Sunday Two shows a day
Bobby Bare she said with a shake
of her head *Just what the hell*
are you doing here And to his credit
Bobby Bare the Elder didn't Ignore her
Roll his eyes Patronize her Pass her off
Didn't pat her on the arm
Flirt Pretend to flirt
Didn't try to pick her up
(From here From now I can see it
I can see my mother was a looker)
Nope Old Bobby Bare
Great American Singer
looked her straight
in the eye Raised his glass
And offered what our family
still uses as a kind of toast
Lady The real question is
What the hell are you
What the hell is anyone
Doing here at all

Kaldi's Goats

Ate the red berries Gamboled
like mad things Chased
their own tails Bit at the air
Out of love Kaldi ate the berries too
Galloped up the hill nine times
Down nine times again
Left his eyes not resting on anything
for long Except the steady gaze
of first one goat Then another
I see said Kaldi *Now I see*

Gathered a handful of the berries
to bring home to his wife She too
grew excited Like Kaldi Like
the goats *This is a gift* she swore
And sent Kaldi to the monastery
Where the monks declared them
of the devil Where the monks
threw them in the fire Where the berries
began to roast Smelled delicious
Pulling all the monks in training
from their cells Kaldi scooped

the berries from the fire Rescued
what remained Dropped the warm
beans into the goatskin he carried
with him full of water
From God he said *For me*

Sipping at the water Kaldi made it home
that evening in time to say
his night prayers Knew his wife
Her warm embrace Talked of
a future How 4 goats might become
8 The life 8 goats offers A man His wife
They rose together to gaze
upon the sleeping goats
To goggle the stars above
The wonders hidden
by the dark The miracle in living
Eyes open at last to see them

Amo Amas Amat Amamus

Love is a crazy old thing
And one night you will find yourself
on your knees praying
Jesus Please don't let me kill her
If I go to jail it's going to break
my mother's heart

But the truth is you should be thankful
for an opportunity to fall to your knees and pray
for the patience not to kill the one you love
because that is one way to know you are in love and alive

For the secret to love is The other person's craziness
can't make you crazy You are never going to find somebody
who isn't crazy So you need to work on finding someone
who when everyone else thinks *Lord I could never*
live with that leaves you thinking *Don't worry baby*
To me you're fine Just fine

The art of loving the crazy
I learned from my family Like a gift

handed down generation to generation
Take for instance People like my grandfather
A farmer who worked in the fields everyday
Wore the same type of clunky old shoes
I do now and would at every possible opportunity
Swear to you that we had never really landed
on the moon *It's the desert* he'd say *Anyone*
could tell if they would just look closely
I can't believe they ever thought we would all
be that easy to fool But he was wrong
We are It happens everyday

Take for instance When my grandfather died
My mother leaned over the casket
and kissed him full on the lips
and I thought *I will never love anyone*
enough to do that and *I may never kiss*
my mother again But I was wrong
And I remembered how wrong I was
years later when I looked out the window
of a plane and watched them load
my mother's casket into the hold below

At that moment all I wanted to do was
Walk right back out the plane's little umbilical cord
March my clunky boots up the narrow stairs
to where they store all the gas and the food and the luggage
and Curl up next to her because I thought
It must be cold down there

And lonely too And that
is no way to go back home

And it is hard to find someone who understands things
Like grandfathers believing moon landings were faked
Or a person wanting to fly across the country
in the frozen airless womb of a plane
so her already dead mother won't be lonely
or scared And even I will admit These things
are crazy Crazier in many ways than just
Kissing the dead But I also have hope
that someday I will find someone
who will love me For these things
Not despite them Because

Love is a crazy old thing
And one night you will find yourself
on your knees praying
Jesus Thank you for not letting me kill her
If she weren't around it would break my heart

The fact that Jesus or whoever granted you the patience
not to kill the one you love probably means that person
has been down on their knees
praying for the strength to deal with you as well
and that may be one way to know they love you too

For the secret to love is Your craziness
can't make the other person crazy You are never

going to not be crazy So you need to work on finding somebody

who when everyone else thinks *Lord that girl*

is crazy will put her arm around your shoulder

and whisper in your ear *Don't worry baby*

I think you're fine Just fine

flower of the mountain

longest living marrieds man say
dont seem like it but he say one of the last
longest livings gone now it us he say
we the longest living marrieds now
whats your trick he say dont go to bed mad
that aint a trick aint a trick to it
stay living stay married stay stay
and you done it a man call you
say now you the longest living marrieds

it hard he say married aint hard
married just staying but staying
aint not leaving to stay you got
to stay man drifting downriver on a log
aint leaving that log but he aint stay
my man river captain know every
stuckup bit of land every eddy
my man stay that river so long
times it like he married that river
maybe river and my man
next longest living marrieds

he say you finish each other sentence
how he think that married how he think
I know what my man say man open
his mouth foolish crawl out every day
married aint finishing sentences them
Chinese brothers joined at the heart
finished they other sentence we seen them
up the fair sitting joined walking joined
one died right after the other cause they
shared blood them boys had no choice
they nothing like marrieds

how you do it he say times choose marriage
each day some days choose each minute
chose it this morning choosing it
right now choosing how he asked
said theres many he could choose
and many would choose me I think
Lord he going to do it right here
atop the colored wheel at Seabreeze

he take my hand and the wheel go up
I see them Chinese brothers and think *stuck*
he say what you say I think he a river captain
he come he go he already choose he choose river
he say I choose you you my mountain flower
we top the wheel now I ask him ask right
he say you do me the honor and I think
just now no one know but me

the wheel break over the top stop

look out over Seabreeze

tallest I been since I left home see people

I never see again I say yes

he say yes that wheel start down

he say seeing them joined boys good luck

this time wheel go round dont stop

man today say tell everyone

your story I say we atop a wheel

and I seen it all he say Zelmyra

say yes I say yes

and the big wheel spin top the fair

I seen it all ocean mountain river swamp yes

the wheel go round while you sit still

Oh Lord yes it most certainly

do yes it still do

NOTES

Zeno's Boat includes a version of Isiah 1:18

o camerado close! o you and me at last is a quotation from Walt Whitman's *Starting From Paumanok* in the 3ʳᵈ edition of *Leaves of Grass*. The poem also contains a line from Whitman's *Song of Myself* Section VI, sometimes referred to as *A child said, What is the Grass?*

ever you desire was written in response to Geffrey Davis's *The Fidelity of Light* as part of *At Length* magazine's Telephone Project. As well, the poem contains lyrics from the Bob Marley and the Wailers song *War*

Sometimes Birds Spontaneously contains lyrics from the folk song *God Gave Noah The Rainbow Sign*

54 Prince contains lyrics from the folk song *Worried Man Blues*

Things Like Words Words Like Things includes 2 lines from Emily Dickinson's *It might be lonelier/Without the Loneliness*

Other People Call It America includes lines from Fannie Lou Hamer's 1964 speech to the Credentials Committee at the Democratic National Convention. Hamer spoke as vice-chair of the Mississippi Freedom Democratic Party

The poem also contains lines from (*You Make Me Feel Like*) *A Natural Woman*, a song written by Carole King and Gerry Goffin and first recorded by Aretha Franklin, and *My Country 'Tis Of Thee (America)* by Samuel Francis Smith

Someday I'll Love Ocean Vuong contains lyrics from a folk song, known either as *My Father Was A Gambler* or *I've Been All Around This World*

Bobby Bare quotes Bobby Bare, Jr. from a *Chicago Tribune* interview with Andy Dowling on May 26, 2006

flower of the mountain takes its title and form from the Molly Bloom chapter of James Joyce's *Ulysses*

ACKNOWLEDGMENTS

Earlier versions of the following poems previously appeared in the following journals. Thanks go to their editors for giving them their first home; special thanks go to the editors at *Red Rock Review* and *at length* for feedback and edits that ultimately made the poems stronger.

"54 Prince" appeared in *The Awl* and was included in *Best American Poetry 2015*

"o camerado close" appeared in *Abundant Grace*

"flower of the mountain" appeared in *Beloit Poetry Journal*

"Zeno's Boat" appeared in *Forklift, Ohio*

"Never Never Pants" appeared in *H_NGM_N*

"txt me im board" appeared in *at length*

"Son of a Son of a Son" appeared in *Red Rock Review*

THANKS

I have appreciation for members of the Black Socks poetry group; their feedback and support helped some of these poems come to their final versions.

As well, thanks go to VCCA for 2 weeks that allowed me to do the final work on this book.

I am indebted to the CURRENTS: Humanities Work Now series at UMBC's Drescher Center and to my colleague Lia Purpura; both provided important opportunities to try out versions of *txt me im board* with readers.

Special love goes to Ocean Vuong, who graciously read a manuscript version of *Stay*. His thoughtful feedback made the book and individual poems better; his steadfast friendship makes me better.

Appreciation, love, and gratitude go to everyone at YesYes Books, but especially KMA Sullivan, editor and leader extraordinaire. Her work on *Boyishly* and *Stay*, not to mention her day-to-day efforts to respect poets and poetry, put YesYes at the head of the publishing pack. There may be bigger presses, but there are none better.

A special kind of love is offered for my family—my parents, whom I miss every day, each in their own way; my sister, who never gives up; my nephew, who teaches me so much about how to be a good, steadfast friend; my aunts, uncles, and cousins who love me and allow me to love in turn.

Finally, all my love goes to Susan Pietrzyk. Despite my poetic moodiness, inability to pick up my shoes, occasional grouchiness, and many other shortcomings, she stays.

TANYA OLSON lives in Silver Spring, Maryland and is a Senior Lecturer in English at University of Maryland Baltimore County (UMBC). Her first book, *Boyishly*, was awarded a 2014 American Book Award and her second book, *Stay*, was released from YesYes Books in 2019. She was a Discovery Poetry Contest winner from *Boston Review* and the 92nd Street Y and is a Lambda Fellow of the Writers Retreat for Emerging LGBTQ Voices.

Also from YesYes Books

some planet by jamie mortara

Boyishly by Tanya Olson

a falling knife has no handle by Emily O'Neill

Pelican by Emily O'Neill

The Youngest Butcher in Illinois by Robert Ostrom

A New Language for Falling Out of Love by Meghan Privitello

I'm So Fine: A List of Famous Men & What I Had On by Khadijah Queen

American Barricade by Danniel Schoonebeek

The Anatomist by Taryn Schwilling

Gilt by Raena Shirali

Panic Attack, USA by Nate Slawson

[insert] boy by Danez Smith

Man vs Sky by Corey Zeller

The Bones of Us by J. Bradley
   [Art by Adam Scott Mazer]

CHAPBOOK COLLECTIONS

Vinyl 45s

   After by Fatimah Asghar

   Inside My Electric City by Caylin Capra-Thomas

   Dream with a Glass Chamber by Aricka Foreman

   Exit Pastoral by Aidan Forster

   Pepper Girl by Jonterri Gadson

   Of Darkness and Tumbling by Mónica Gomery

   Bad Star by Rebecca Hazelton

   Makeshift Cathedral by Peter LaBerge

   Still, the Shore by Keith Leonard

   Please Don't Leave Me Scarlett Johansson by Thomas Patrick Levy

   Juned by Jenn Marie Nunes

A History of Flamboyance by Justin Phillip Reed

Unmonstrous by John Allen Taylor

Giantess by Emily Vizzo

No by Ocean Vuong

This American Ghost by Michael Wasson

Blue Note Editions

   Beastgirl & Other Origin Myths by Elizabeth Acevedo

   Kissing Caskets by Mahogany L. Browne

   One Above One Below: Positions & Lamentations by Gala Mukomolova

Companion Series

   Inadequate Grave by Brandon Courtney

   The Rest of the Body by Jay Deshpande